True Credit Restoration
A Guide To Repairing Your Credit The Right Way.

By Alisha Allen

1

Table of Contents

Introduction

There are many misconceptions about credit scores out there. Some customers believe that they don't have a credit score and many customers who think that their credit scores just don't really matter. These sorts of misconceptions can hurt your chances at some jobs, at reasonable interest rates, and even your chances of getting some apartments.

The truth is, if you have a bank account and bills, then you have a credit score, and your credit score matters more than you might think. Your credit score may be called many things, including a credit risk rating, a FICO score, a credit rating, a FICO rating, or a credit risk score. All these terms refer to the same thing: the three-digit number that lets lenders get an idea of how likely you are to repay your bills.

Every time you apply for credit, apply for a job that requires you to handle money, or even apply for some more exclusive types of living apartment, your credit score is checked.

In fact, your credit score can be checked by anyone with a legitimate business need to do so. Your credit score is based on your past financial responsibilities and past payments and credit, and it provides potential lenders with a quick snapshot of your current financial state and past repayment habits.

In other words, your credit score lets lenders know quickly how much of a credit risk you are. Based on this credit score, lenders decide whether to trust you financially - and give you better rates when you apply for a loan. Apartment managers can use your credit score to determine if you can be trusted to pay your rent on time. Employers can use your credit score to decide whether you can be trusted in a high-responsibility job that requires you to handle money.

The problem with credit scores is that there is quite a bit of misinformation circulated about, mainly through some less than scrupulous companies who claim they can help you with your credit report and credit score - for a cost, of course.

From advertisements and suspect claims, customers

sometimes come away with the idea that in order to boost their credit score, they have to pay money to a company or leave credit repair in the hands of so-called "experts." Nothing could be further from the truth. It is perfectly possible to pay down debts and boost your credit on your own, with no expensive help whatsoever.

In fact, the following 101 tips can get you well on your way to boosting your credit score and saving you money.

By the end of this book, you will be able to:

•Define a credit score, a credit report, and other key financial terms

•Develop a personalized credit repair plan that addresses your unique financial situation

•Find the resources and people who can help you repair your credit score

•Repair your credit effectively using the very techniques used by credit repair experts

Plus, unlike many other books on the subject, this book will show you how to deal with your everyday life while repairing your credit. Your credit repair does not happen in a vacuum.

This book will teach you the powerful strategies you need to build the financial habits that will help you keep a high credit risk rating. It really is that simple.

Start reading and be prepared to start taking small but powerful steps that can have a dramatic impact on your financial life!

Chapter 1
The Basics

Before you start boosting your credit score, you need to know the basics. You need to know what a credit score is, how it is developed, and why it is important to you in your everyday life.

Lenders certainly know what sort of information they can get from a credit score, but knowing this information yourself can help you better see how your everyday financial decisions impact the financial picture lenders get of you through your credit score. A few simple tips are all you need to know to understand the basic principles:

Understand Your Credit Scores

If you are going to improve your credit score, then logic has it that you must understand what your credit score is and how it works. Without this information, you won't be able to improve your score very effectively because you won't understand how the things you do in life daily affect your score.

If you don't understand how your credit score works, you will also be at the mercy of any company that tries to tell you how you can improve your score - on their terms and at their price.

In general, your credit score is a number that lets lenders know how much of a credit risk you are. The credit score is a number, usually between 300 and 850, that allows lenders know how well you are paying off your debts and how much of a credit risk you are.

In general, the higher your credit score, the better credit risk you make and the more likely you are to be given credit at great rates. Scores in the low 600s and below will often give you trouble in finding credit, while scores of 720 and above will generally give you the best interest rates out there. However, credit scores are a lot like GPAs or SAT scores from college days - while they give others a quick snapshot of how you are doing, they are interpreted by people in different ways. Some lenders put more emphasis on credit scores than others.

Some lenders will work with you if you have credit scores in the 600s, while others offer their best rates only to those creditors with very high scores indeed. Some lenders will look at your entire credit report while others will accept or reject your loan application based solely on your credit score.

The credit score is based on your credit report, which contains a history of your past debts and repayments. Credit bureaus use computers and mathematical calculations to arrive at a credit score from the information contained in your credit report.

Each credit bureau uses different methods to do this (which is why you will have different scores with different companies), but most credit bureaus use the FICO system. FICO is an acronym for the credit score calculating software offered by Fair Isaac Corporation company. This is by far the most used software since the Fair Isaac Corporation developed the credit score model used by many in the financial industry and is still considered one of the leaders in the field.

In fact, credit scores are sometimes called FICO scores or FICO ratings, although it is important to understand that your score may be tabulated using different software.

One other thing you may want to understand about the software and mathematics that goes into your credit score is the fact that the math used by the software is based on research and comparative mathematics. This is an important and simple concept that can help you understand how to boost your credit score. In simple terms, what this means is that your credit score is in a way calculated on the same principles as your insurance premiums.

Your insurance company likely asks you questions about your health, your lifestyle choices (such as whether you are a smoker) because these bits of information can tell the insurance company how much of a risk you are and how likely you are to make large claims later on. This is based on research.

Studies have shown, for example, that smokers tend to be more prone to severe illnesses and so require more medical attention. If you are a smoker, you may face higher insurance premiums because of this.

Similarly, credit bureaus and lenders often look at general patterns. Since people with too many debts tend not to have great rates of repayment, your credit score may suffer if you have too many debts, for example. Understanding this can help you in two ways:

1) It will let you see that your credit score is not a personal reflection of how "good" or "bad" you are with money. Instead, it is a reflection of how well lenders and companies think you will repay your bills - based on information gathered from studying other people.

2) It will let you see that if you want to improve your credit score, you need to work on becoming the sort of debtor that studies have shown tends to repay their bills. You do not have to work hard to reinvent yourself financially, and you do not have to start making much more money. You just need to be a reliable lender. This realization alone should help make credit repair far less stressful!

Credit reports are put together by credit bureaus, which use information from client companies. It works like this: credit bureaus have clients - such as credit card companies and utility companies, to name just two - who provide them with information.

Once a file is begun on you (i.e., once you open a bank account or have bills to pay) then information about you is stored on the record. If you are late paying a bill, the clients call the credit bureaus and note this. Any unpaid bills, overdue bills or other problems with credit count as "dings" on your credit report and affect your score.

Information such as what type of debt you have, how much debt you have, how regularly you pay your bills on time, and your credit accounts are all information that is used to calculate your credit score.

Your age, sex, and income do not count towards your credit score. The actual formula used by credit bureaus to calculate credit scores is a well-kept secret, but it is known that recent account activity, debts, length of credit, unpaid accounts, and types of credit are among the things that count the most in tabulating credit scores from a credit report.

Contact Info for Credit Bureaus

The three major credit bureaus are important to contact if you are going to be repairing your credit score. The major three credit agencies can help you by sending you your credit report. If you find an error on your credit report, these are also the companies you must contact in order to correct the problem. You can easily contact these organizations by mail, telephone, or through the Internet:

Equifax Credit Information Services, Inc
Address: P.O. Box 740241
       Atlanta, GA 30374
Telephone: 1_888_766_0008
Online: www.equifax.com

TransUnion LLC Consumer Disclosure Center
Address: P.O. Box 1000
       Chester, PA 19022
Telephone: 1_800_888_4213
Online: www.tuc.com

Experian National Consumer Assistance Center

Address: PO Box 2002

Allen, TX 75013

Telephone: 1_888_397_3742

Online: www.experian.com

You may want to note this information wherever most of your financial information is kept so that you can easily contact the bureaus whenever you need to. Your local yellow pages should also have the contact information of these credit agencies as well.

An Action Plan for Dealing With Your Credit Score

Once you have your credit report and your credit score, you will be able to tell where you stand and where many of your problems lie. If you have a poor score, try to see on your credit report what could be causing the problem:

-Do you have too much debt?

-Too many unpaid bills?

-Have you recently faced a major financial upset such as a bankruptcy?

-Have you simply not had credit long enough to establish

good credit?

-Have you defaulted on a loan, failed to pay taxes, or recently been reported to a collection agency?

The problems that contribute to your credit problems should dictate how you decide to boost your credit score. As you read through this book, highlight or jot down those tips that apply to you and from them develop a checklist of things you can do that would help your credit situation improve.

When you seek professional credit counseling or credit help, counselors will generally work with you to help you develop a personalized strategy that expressly addresses your credit problems and financial history. Now, with this book, you can develop a similar strategy on your own - in your own time and at your own cost.

When developing your action plan, know where most of your credit score is coming from:

1) **Your credit history** (accounts for more than a third of your credit score in some cases). Whether or not you have

been a good credit risk in the past is considered the best indicator of how you will react to debt in the future. For this reason, late payment, loan defaults, unpaid taxes, bankruptcies, and other unmet debt responsibilities will count against you the most. You can't do much about your financial past now, but starting to pay your bills on time - starting today - can help boost your credit score in the future.

2) **Your current debts** (accounts for approximately a third of your credit score in some cases). If you have lots of current debt, it may indicate that you are stretching yourself financially thin and so will have trouble paying back debts in the future. If you have a lot of money owing right now - and especially if you have borrowed a great deal recently - this fact will bring down your credit score. You can boost your credit score by paying down your debts as far as you can.

3) **How long you have had credit** (accounts for up to 15% of your credit score in some cases). If you have not had credit accounts for very long, you may not have enough of a history to let lenders know whether you make a good

credit risk. Not having had credit for a long time can affect your credit score. You can counter this by keeping your accounts open rather than closing them off as you pay them off.

4) **The types of credit you have** (accounts for about one-tenth of your credit score, in most cases). Lenders like to see a mix of financial responsibilities that you handled well. Having bills that you pay as well as one or two types of loans can improve your credit score. Having at least one credit card that you manage well can also help your credit score.

As you can see, it is possible to only estimate how much a specific area of your credit report affects your credit score. Nevertheless, keeping these five areas in mind and making sure that each is addressed in your personalized plan will go a long way in making sure that your personalized credit repair plan is comprehensive enough to boost your credit efficiently.

Chapter 2

Boost Your Credit Score

Because of the way credit scores are calculated, some actions you take will affect your credit score better than others. In general, paying your bills on time and meeting your financial responsibilities will boost your score the most. Owing a reasonable amount of money and being able to repay it will show lenders that you take your finances seriously and pose little threat to lost money. There are a few tips that, more than any other, will boost your credit score the most:

Pay Your Bills on Time.

One of the best ways to improve your credit score is simply to pay your bills on time. This is absurdly simple, but it works very well because nothing shows lenders that you take debts seriously as much as a history of paying promptly. Every lender wants to be paid in full and on time.

If you pay all your bills on time, then the odds are good that you will make the payments on a new debt on time too, and that is indeed something every lender wants to see. Experts think that up to 35% of your credit score is based on your paying off bills on time, so this simple step is one of the easiest ways to boost your credit score.

Paying your bills on time also ensures that you don't get hit with late fees and other financial penalties that make paying your bills off harder. Paying your bills in a timely way makes it easier to keep making payments on time.

Of course, if you have had problems making your payments on time in the past, your current credit score will reflect this. It will take a number of months of repaying your bills on time to improve your credit score again, but the effort will be well worth it when your credit risk rating rebounds!

Avoid Excessive Credit

If you have many lines of credit or several huge debts, you make a worse credit risk because you are close to "overextending your credit." This simply means that you may be taking on more credit than you can comfortably pay off. Even if you are making payments regularly now on existing bills, lenders know that you will have a harder time paying off your bills if your debt load grows too much.

The higher your debts, the greater your monthly debt payments and so the higher the risk that you will eventually be able to repay your debts. Plus, statistical studies have shown that those with high debt loads have the hardest time financially when faced with a crisis such as a divorce, unemployment, or sudden illness.

Lenders (and credit bureaus who calculate your credit score) know that the more debt you have, the greater problems, you will have in case you do run into a life crisis.

In order to have a great credit score, avoid taking out excessive credit. You should stick to one or two credit cards and one or two other major debts (car loan, mortgage) to have the best credit rating. Do not apply for every new credit line or credit card "just in case." Borrow only when you need it and make sure to make payments on your debts on time.

You should also know that taking out lots of new credit accounts in a relatively short period of time will cause your credit score to nosedive because it will look as though you are financially irresponsible.

Pay Down Your Debts

If you have a lot of debt, your credit score will suffer. Paying down your debts to a minimum will help elevate your credit score. For example, if you have a $1000 limit on your credit card and you regularly carry a balance of $900, you will be a less attractive credit risk to lenders than someone who has the same credit card but carries a smaller balance of $100 or so. If you are serious about improving your credit score, then start with the largest debt you have and start paying it down so that you are using a less large percentage of your credit total.

In general, try to make sure that you use no more than 50% of your credit. That means that if your credit card has a limit of $5000, make sure that you pay it down to at least $2500 and work at carrying no larger balance. If possible, reduce the debt even more. If you can pay off your credit card in full each month, that is even better. What counts here is what percentage of your total credit limit you are using - the lower, the better.

A Range of Credit Types

The types of credit you have are a factor in calculating your credit score. In general, lenders like to see that you are able to handle a range of credit types well. Having some form of personal credit - such as credit cards - and some larger types of credit - such as a mortgage or auto loan - and paying them off regularly is better than having only one type of credit.

Chapter 3

Keep Your Score Safe

If you have a lower credit score that you would like, odds are that the score is caused by some small financial mistake or oversight you have made in the past. Not every person with bad credit has a low credit score caused by something they did, though. Sometimes, other people's criminal activity can affect your credit score. There are a few tips that can keep you and your credit safe from online and financial predators:

Look Out for Identity Theft

Many people who are careful about paying bills on time and having minimal debts are shocked each year to find that they have low credit scores. In many cases, this happens as a result of identity theft. Identity theft is a type of crime in which people take your personal information and steal that information to pose as you in order to get access to your accounts or identity

For example, someone with your PIN numbers can remove small amounts of money from your bank account each month, or someone can use your name and personal information to get credit cards in your name and use those credit cards with no intention of paying back the money. You are stuck with the massive debts and the poor credit score.

To prevent identity theft, always check your account statements carefully each month. Report any suspicious activity or any charges you don't recognize at once. Also, check your credit report regularly and immediately investigate any new credit accounts you do not recognize - this is the best way of detecting and acting on identity theft.

If you have been the victim of identity theft, report to the police at once and get a police statement. Send copies of this to your bank and credit bureaus. Better yet, get the credit bureaus to attach the report to your credit report if you can. Close all your accounts and reopen new ones. You should not have to pay for someone else's illegal activity.

Safe Practices

To stay safe from identity theft, always follow secure banking and financial practices:

1) Keep account numbers and PIN numbers safe. Cover your account and PIN numbers when using debit at the store and refuse to give your PIN number to anyone. Avoid writing down your PIN and account numbers - you never know when this information could fall into the wrong hands.

2) Only do business with businesses you trust.

3)If you get applications for credit cards in the mail that are "pre-approved" rip up the applications and enclosed letters before discarding them. No, this is not paranoid. Identity thieves sometimes go through garbage in order to find these forms so that they can fill them out and steal your identity.

4) If you use a computer, install good firewall and antivirus protection system and update it religiously. Better yet, take a course in safe computing at your local college or

community center. You will learn many useful tips for keeping all your information safe while you are online.

5) Never buy anything online from a company you do not trust or from a company that does not have encryption technology and good privacy policy.

6) Even with all computer precautions, avoid providing private information through email on your computer. Be especially cautious if you get an email from your bank asking you to verify your information by clicking on a link - this is a popular scam that comes not from your bank but criminals posing as your bank. Ignore the email and phone your bank about the message.

7) Be wary of unsolicited emails, phone calls, or mail advertisements. Most are from legitimate companies, but some companies promise you a credit card over the telephone only to charge your existing credit card without sending you anything.

Similarly, letters will sometimes promise you specific items or services. Once you send in your credit card information (usually to a post office box), you hear no more from the company. If you need or want to buy something from a company, be sure to check the company's standing with the Better Business Bureau first.

Send a money order instead of a check (which had your account number) or your credit card information. If you do use a credit card, report any unusual charges or any payments you made for a product that did not arrive at the credit card company.

In some cases, they can stop payment or refund your money as well as take steps to keep your credit card number safe.

8) Be wary of offers that seem too good to be true. If you get an offer for a ten-million-dollar check - for which you need to put down $5000 as a "sign of good faith" ...if you get an offer for a free state-of-the-art computer - if only you provide your account information... take a deep breath and consider before sending in your money and your information.

Offers that are too good to be true always are. Scam artists often rely on your belief in others and your trust to make money. They depend on the fact that you will be so excited about a product or service that you will throw good judgment out the window. Prove them wrong.

When faced with an offer that seems too good to be true, do some research on the web, through the Better Business Bureau, or ask the person making the offer some questions. Never take someone up on an offer that you have been given unsolicited unless the company and the offer both check out.

9) Read the fine print. Some services or companies will have tiny print in their contract or agreement that allows them to charge you extra hidden fees or that allows them to retract certain offers. If you get an offer through email or the mail, make it a habit of reading the fine print.

10) Be alert for a sudden disruption in your mail service. If you do not get mail for some time, contact your post office and ask whether your address was recently submitted for a "change of address" service. It sounds strange, but it's true.

One way that criminals steal identities is to change your address at the local post office. They redirect your mail to a post office box number and steal your mail looking for personal information such as bank statements, pre-approved credit card applications, and other pieces of mail they can use to steal your identity.

They use this information to pose as you to lenders and run up huge charges in your name. Simply keeping an eye out on your mail can help you keep your credit score safe.

Check Your Credit Score Regularly

You are more likely to notice problems and inconsistencies if you check your credit score on a regular basis - at least once a year and preferably three times a year. Be sure to check your credit rating with each credit bureau, too. If you notice anything odd or anything you don't recognize (such as a charge account, you did not open) report it immediately.

Sometimes, these errors are caused by mistakes made at the

credit bureau, but they could be an indication that someone is using your identity. In either case, such mistakes could hurt your credit score. Fixing such errors improves your credit score.

If you think you have been the victim of identity theft, take action at once:

1) Contact the three major credit bureaus and ask to speak to the fraud department. Explain that you have been the victim of identity theft (or believe you may have been) and request that an "alert" be placed on your file. This will let anyone looking at your report know that you may have been the victim of fraud. It will also mean that you will be alerted any time a lender asks to look at your file - each time a lender does look at your file, it may be an indication that the identity thieves are trying to open a new account in your name.

When the lender sees that the person applying is not you, they will deny the thieves credit, and in most cases, the criminals will stop trying to access your identity. Most alerts on your file last 90 or 180 days but you can extend this period to several years by asking the credit agencies for an extension of the "fraud alert" in writing.

In some states, you can even ask for a freeze to be placed on your credit score and credit report which will prevent anyone but yourself and those creditors you already have from accessing your file. Any lenders the thieves contact to set up a new account will be refused access, and the thieves will not be able to get any more money in your name.

You are entitled to a free copy of your credit report if you have been the victim of identity theft. Be sure to take advantage of this offer so that you can check exactly how your credit has been affected. Dispute those items that are not yours.

2) Call the Federal Trade Commission (FTC) at 1-877-438-4338. This is the special hotline that the FTC has set up to help customers deal with fraud and identity theft. You will be able to get up-to-date information about your rights and advice as to what you can do to improve your credit score and keep it safe in the future.

3) Contact the police. Identity theft is a crime, and you

need to file a police report (be sure to keep a copy of this report) so that you can help the police potentially catch the criminals responsible. Contacting the police will also give you a paper trail and proof that a crime has been committed. Keeping a paper trail of the crime and your response will make it easier for you to repair your credit if it has been damaged by identity thieves.

4) Contact your creditors or any creditors that the identity thieves have opened an account with. Ask to speak to the security department and explain your predicament. You may need to have your accounts closed or at least your passwords changed to protect yourself.

You may also need to fill out a fraud affidavit to state that a crime has been committed - be sure to keep a copy of this form for your records. The security team of the creditors should be able to advise you as to what you can do. Be sure to note down who you contacted and when so that you have records of the steps you have taken to deal with the crime.

If you have been the victim of identity theft and you are

deeply in debt to creditors you never contacted, you will not be held responsible for the charges - but you will have to prove that you have been the victim of identity theft, which is tricky since the thieves are using your name and claiming to be you.

It is a frustrating experience because lenders will want to be paid and you will want to avoid paying for charges you did not run up. Being persistent and keeping good proof that you have been the victim of a crime will help to clear your credit score. In the meantime, however, you will be faced with a much lower credit rating than you deserve, and you may have to put off larger purchases that may require a loan.

Chapter 4

Common Credit Mistakes

There are a few things that people do without realizing that it will have a bad effect on their credit score. Follow these tips to avoid the common traps that can sink your credit risk rating:

Beware of Debts And Credit You Don't Use

It is easy today to apply for a store credit card that you forget all about in three years - but that account will remain on your credit report and affect your credit score as long as it is open. Having credit lines and credit cards you don't need makes you seem like a worse credit risk because you run the risk of "overextending" your credit.

Also, having lots of accounts you don't use increases the odds that you will forget about an old account and stop making payments on it - resulting in a lowered credit score. Keep only your used accounts and make sure that all other accounts are closed. Having fewer accounts will make it easier for you to keep track of your debts and will increase the chances of you having a good credit score.

However, realize that when you close an account, the record of the closed account remains on your credit report and can affect your credit score for a while. In fact, closing unused credit accounts may cause your credit score to drop in the short term, as you will have higher credit balances spread out over a smaller overall credit account base.

For example, if your unused accounts amounted to $2000 and you owe $1000 on accounts that you have now (let's say on two credit cards that total $2000) you have gone from using one-fourth of your credit ($1000 owed on a possible $4000 you could have borrowed) to using one-half of your credit (you owe $1000 from a possible $2000). This will cause your credit risk rating to drop. In the long term, though, not having extra temptation to charge and not having credit you don't need can work for you.

Be Careful of Inquiries on Your Credit Report

Every time that someone looks at your credit report, the inquiry is noted. If you have lots of inquiries on your report, it may appear that you are shopping for several loans at once - or that you have been rejected by lenders. Both make you appear a poor credit risk and may affect your credit score. This means that you should be careful about who looks at your credit report. If you are shopping for a loan, shop around within a short period of time, since inquiries made within a few days of each other will generally be lumped together and counted as one inquiry.

You can also cut down on the number of inquiries on your account by approaching lenders you have already researched and may be interest in doing business with - by researching first and approaching second you will likely have only a few lenders accessing your credit report at the same time, which can help save your credit score.

Be Careful of Online Loan Rate Comparisons

Online loan rate quotes are easy to get - type in some personal information, and you can get a quote on your car loan, personal loan, student loan, or mortgage in seconds. This is free and convenient, leading many people to compare several companies at once to make sure that they get the best deal possible.

The problem is that since online quotes are a fairly recent phenomenon, credit bureaus count each such quote estimate as an "inquiry." This means that if you compare too many companies online by asking for quotes, your credit score will fall due to too many "inquiries."

This does not mean that you shouldn't seek online quotes for loans - not at all. In fact, online loan quotes are a great resource that can help you get the very best rates on your next loan. What this information does mean, however, is that you should research companies and narrow down possible lenders to just a few before making inquiries. This will help ensure that the number of inquiries on your credit report is small - and your credit rating will stay in good shape.

Don't Make the Mistake of Thinking That You Only Have One Credit Report

Most people speak of having a "credit score" when in fact most people have at least three or more scores - and these scores can vary widely. There are three major credit bureaus in the country that develop credit reports and calculate credit scores. There are also several smaller credit bureau companies.

Plus, some larger lenders calculate their own credit risk scores based on information on your credit report. When repairing your credit score, then, you should not focus on one number - at the very least, you need to contact the three major credit bureaus and work on repairing the three credit scores separately.

Don't Make the Mistake of Closing Lots of Credit Accounts Just To Improve Your Score.

This seems like a contradiction, but it really is not. Many people think that to improve their credit score, they just have to pay off some debts and close their accounts. This is not exactly accurate. There are several reasons to think carefully before closing your accounts.

First, if you close an account you need (for example, if you close all your credit card accounts) then you will have to reapply for credit, and all those inquiries from lenders will cause your credit score to drop.

Secondly, most credit bureaus give high favorable points to those who have an excellent long-term credit history. That means that closing the credit card account, you have had since college may hurt you in the long run. If you have credit accounts that you don't use or if you have too many credit lines, then pay off some and close them. Doing so may help your credit score - but only if you don't close long-term accounts you need. In general, close the most recent accounts first and only when you are sure you will not need that credit in the near future. Closing your accounts is a bad idea if:

1) You will be applying for a loan soon. The closing of your accounts will make your credit score drop in the short term and will not allow you to qualify for reasonable loan rates.

2) Closing your accounts will make your overall debt

balance too high. If you owe $10 000 now and closing some accounts would leave you with only $1000 of possible credit, you are close to maxing out your credit - which gives you a bad credit rating.

In the short term, closing accounts will lower your credit score, but in the long run, it can be beneficial.

Don't Assume That One Thing Will Boost Your Credit Score a Specific Number Of Points

Some debtors are lead to believe that paying off a credit card bill will boost their credit score by 50 points while closing an unused credit account will result in 20 more points. Credit scores are certainly not this clear-cut or simple.

How much any one action will affect your credit score is impossible to gauge. It will depend on several factors, including your current credit score and the credit bureau calculating your credit score.

In general, though, the higher your credit score, the smaller factors - such as one unpaid bill - can affect you. However, when repairing your credit score, you should not be equating specific credit repair tasks with numbers. The idea is to do as many things as you can to get your credit score as close to 800 as you are able. Even if you can improve your credit score by 100 points or so, you will qualify for better interest rates.

Don't Think That Having No Loans or Debts Will Improve Your Credit Score

Some people believe that owing no money, having no credit cards, and in fact, avoiding the whole world of credit will help improve their credit score. The opposite is true - lenders want to see that you can handle credit, and the only way they can tell is if you have credit that you managed responsibly. Having no credit at all can be worse for your credit score than having a few credit accounts that you pay off scrupulously. If you currently have no credit accounts at all, opening a low balance credit card can boost your credit score.

Never Do Anything Illegal to Help Boost Your Credit Score

It seems obvious, but plenty of people try to lie about their credit scores or even falsify their loan applications because they are ashamed of a bad score. Not only is this illegal, but it is also completely ineffective. Your credit score is easy to check and not only will you not fool lenders by lying but you may find yourself facing legal action because of your dishonesty.

Chapter 5
Your Credit Report

If you want to improve your credit score, you need to go right to the source - your credit report. Your credit report contains the information and data on which your credit score is based. If you can alter or update the information on your credit report, your credit score will change to reflect the alterations. For this reason, getting and checking your credit report is one of the first things you should do when you attempt to repair your credit score. There are a few tips that can help you deal with your credit report so that you can give your credit score a boost:

Dispute Errors on Your Credit Report

Contact each of the three major credit bureaus - TransUnion, Equifax, and Experian - and get copies of your credit reports and credit scores. Carefully read over the reports and note any errors. In writing, contact the credit bureaus and ask that mistakes be removed or investigated.

This is called a dispute letter, and once it is received, credit bureaus must investigate your dispute within thirty days of receiving your letter. It is important to keep a copy of your letter, and it is important to note the date the letter was sent. You should not be accusatory or abusive in your letter - calmly and clearly state the problem and request an investigation.

Note that you are aware the agency is required to investigate the claim within thirty days and note that you will follow up. Be sure that you do follow up with the issues you raised in your letter - just because the agency investigates does not always mean that your credit report will end up error-free.

Many credit bureaus now make it possible for you to correct errors on your credit report online - and many have information on their websites that tell you exactly how disputes must be handled to be effectively removed. It is important that you follow this information exactly so that the inaccuracies on your credit report are removed promptly, and your credit score is updated as soon as possible.

Add A Note to Your Credit Report If There Is A Problem You Can't Resolve

Sometimes, there are legitimate reasons why you didn't pay a bill. If a contractor refused to finish a job or did a poor job, then you may have refused payment, but the non-payment may still count against you on your credit report. If there are any unusual circumstances surrounding your credit report that may affect your credit rating - such as a case of identity theft - you can ask that a note be attached to your credit report to explain the problem.

Some lenders will pay attention to this and some will not, but it is a better solution than nothing at all. Such a note will not affect your credit score but will affect your credit report. More importantly, it leaves a paper trail of the problem that lenders can look at if they choose.

Make Sure You Know Who Is Looking at Your Credit Report And Why

Many inquiries look bad on your credit report, but more

than that you likely want to know who can see your personal financial information, now that you know that your personal information is stored in a credit report. If you sign a document with a lender or apply for credit online, you can be sure that someone is looking at your credit report.

However, you may want to look over other documents to see who is taking a peek. Insurance agents will often look at your credit report, for example. Some landlords and potential employers will, too. You need to be careful about online sources, too. In general, when you provide someone with your social insurance number, you may be giving permission to look at your credit report. You shouldn't bar people from looking, but knowing who is looking is good financial practice.

Know the Difference Between Soft And Hard Inquiries

When you pull your credit report to look at it, it is counted as a "soft inquiry." Only "hard inquiries" from lenders will affect your credit score dramatically. Although checking your credit score too often is an expensive habit, you should not avoid checking your credit report because you fear it will make your credit rating worse.

Contact Creditors as Well As Credit Bureaus When Correcting Inaccuracies in Your Credit Report

When debtors find mistakes on their credit report, they often only contact the credit bureaus. While this is the most efficient way to resolve the issue, you should in some cases contact the creditors whose account has caused a ding on your credit report. This can help future dings and resolve problems faster.

Consider an example: Let's say that you were late sending a credit card payment two months ago because you were sick. The late payment is listed as a ding on your credit report even though you have paid it already. You should contact the credit bureau to get the error removed.

However, if you notice that the same credit card company has you listed as having late payments three months when you paid on time, then it is time to contact the credit company and ask how to resolve the problem.

The information reported about you to credit bureaus should be accurate - if it is not, then the credit company should work to make sure that they correct the problem so that it does not happen again. You have an advantage in this - the credit company, unlike the credit bureau, depends on your business for their money.

This means that the credit company (or any other bill company presenting inaccurate information about you) is well motivated to correct the problem or risk losing you as a client.

If you find that a company consistently reports inaccurate information about you to credit bureaus, consider making a formal complaint to the company about it or switch companies. There is no reason why one company's poor organization should cost you your good credit score.

Look Out Where You Get Your Credit Report - And What It Contains

You can get your credit score from any number of resources. One place you can get it from is from credit bureaus themselves. You can pay for the service, but you qualify for one free credit report a year or qualify for a free credit report if you have recently been turned down for credit or if you think you may have been the victim of identity theft.

If you can, get a copy of your free credit report from each of the three major credit bureaus. If you can't get a free credit report, you should still try to get one, even if costs a few dollars. The savings you will enjoy on your loan rates when you improve your credit score will more than pay for the cost of the reports.

Many online companies offer free online credit reports. These offers are very attractive because you get an online report without having to wait for a report to be sent to you, and you often can get several reports from the different credit bureaus at once, which can save you time. However, these online companies vary widely, so you will want to compare a few different firms before choosing one.

You will also need to read the online company's agreement very carefully - some promise free credit reports only with the purchase of a credit repair program or some other kit. In some cases, you can decline the offer and still get the report but in other cases, you cannot.

Buyer Beware

Also, some companies will offer you free credit reports that are really a combination of reports from the three major credit bureaus. This is not useful since you will want to compare each of the three credit bureau reports and fix each credit score separately. You will want to look out for online companies that offer credit reports that are very condensed, and you will want to avoid companies that will spam you (send you unsolicited emails) trying to get you to subscribe to some service. Always read carefully to see whether the free credit report offer is legitimate.

That said, there are many online companies that offer credit reports and credit scores at no charge, and these can be a useful way for you to start your credit repair, especially if you are comfortable around computers.

If you don't qualify for a free credit report from the credit bureaus, a legitimate online company may be your best bet of getting your credit information so that you can start repairing your credit risk rating.

You do qualify for one free credit report per year. You can get this credit report through email at www.annualcreditreport.com or by calling 877_322_8228.

You can also ask for your free credit report by mail by sending a letter to Annual Credit Report Request Service, P.O. Box 105281, Atlanta, GA 30348_5281 or by filling out the form available at the Federal Trade Commission's Web site at:
http://www.ftc.gov/bcp/conline/edcams/credit/docs/fact_act _request_form.pdf.

No matter where you get your credit score and credit report, make sure that you get the complete information package you can. Credit reports are not very exciting or even easy to read. If you are ordering your report online, look for one that includes graphs or lots of details that are easy to understand.

Make sure that you get both your credit report and your credit score - even if you must pay extra. If you get just your report, you will not be able to follow the secret, and complicated math formulas used to arrive at your score and the report itself will not make as much financial sense to you if you don't have your score in front of you, as well.

When you do get your credit report you will notice that it contains lots of information about you, including:

1) Your personal and contact information. This will include your name and your address, as well as your several past addresses, your social insurance number, your employers (past and present) and your birth date.

2) Your personal information about credit. A credit report notes all the details of your loans, including the types of loans you have now and have recently had, the dates these loans were opened, the credit limit on each loan, how well you have been repaying those loans (this is important - skipped or late payments count heavily against you in your credit score), and who your lenders are.

3) Information about you that is on the public record. This may include bankruptcies, unpaid taxes, unpaid child support, tax liens, your dealings with collection agencies, foreclosures, loan defaults, civil lawsuits that you have been involved in, and other information. Much of this will stay on your credit report and will seriously affect your credit score.

4) Information about who has looked at your credit report and credit score. Every time that someone looks at your credit score it is called an "inquiry." Your credit report lists who has looked at your credit report in the past two years and how often you have applied for loans and credit in that period of time. Too many inquiries tend to look bad and tend to affect your credit score.

When you get your credit report, it is important that you look at all parts of your credit report and understand what you are reading. Mistakes in any area of your credit report can affect your score, so be sure to check the entire report for inaccuracies and errors.

Chapter 6

After a Big Credit Score Problem

Big, bad problems can happen to you - bankruptcies, divorces, lawsuits, non-payment of taxes. These are significant problems that can affect your credit score in a big way. If you have faced a significant problem that has ruined your credit, you need to take action fast and work consistently to boost your FICO score:

If You Have Bad Credit, Establish Better Credit by Taking Out Credit and Repaying It Quickly

If you have terrible credit following a bankruptcy or other major financial upheaval, you may need to get back into an excellent credit rating by taking out a loan you can handle. Make an appointment to see your bank or bad credit lender a few months or years after the problem in question and arrange for a small loan.

You should have enough savings to pay for the loan before you do this. Pay back the loan quickly. It will not hugely boost your credit score, but it will show lenders that you are having an easier time paying your bills. Taking out a small loan you can repay is part of the slow process of reestablishing good credit following a big financial problem.

Try Secured Credit If You Cannot Qualify for Other Types of Credit

Secured credit is credit or a loan which uses something as collateral. In some cases, this could be an asset like a house. In some cases, this collateral could be money frozen in an account by the bank for just such a purchase.

If you need credit following a big problem with your credit score, secured credit may be something you can qualify for. You can use this secured credit to reestablish an excellent credit rating so that you will be eligible for other loans in the future. You may have to pay slightly higher interest if your credit score is quite low, but in the long term repaying this type of loan can improve your credit score.

Give It Time

Many people believe that simply paying off debts will improve their credit score at once. This is not true, unfortunately. If you have experienced a bankruptcy, have been reported to a collection agency, or have had charge-offs, the record will remain on your credit report - even after you have repaid your debts and resolved the problem.

In fact, major problems such as a bankruptcy will remain on your credit report for seven or ten years, affecting your credit score. Even if your credit problems stem from simply not paying bills on time, it will take some time for the mark to fade from your credit report and for your credit score to reflect your better repayment.

Paying off your debts and resolving problems will help your credit score (since overdue accounts will be marked as "paid" on your credit report), but only time will remove the mark of the problems from your record entirely.

This means that if you have faced a major setback such as a bankruptcy, you may have to wait in order to get the best interest rates on larger purchases. The good news is that the further away you are from a major financial problem, the less dire it appears.

For example, if you have declared bankruptcy, you can expect it to have a huge impact on your credit score for the first two years, during which time you will have a hard time getting any credit at all.

However, after two or three years, if you have been paying your bills on time, then the bankruptcy from two years ago will matter less because you have been rebuilding your credit. Your credit will still suffer - but you will slowly be starting to work your way out of the credit problem. Persistence and good financial habits will get you there.

This means that if you plan on making a major purchase (such as a house or car) that may require a loan, you should start working on improving your credit well in advance - even years in advance - of your actual purchase. This is because you simply will not have enough time to radically alter your credit score in time if you wait too long.

Even if your credit score is already reasonably good, you may need to give yourself several months of time to boost your credit rating enough to get the best loan rates.

Contact Your Banks and Ask Credit Limits To Be Reduced

If your credit risk rating is poor, and especially if it has taken a beating lately due to non-payments or other problems, you can ask that your bank reduce the credit limits on your credit cards, credit lines, and other debts. You should do this if:

1) You can pay off at least 50% of your debt loads as they are readjusted. For example, if you have a credit limit of $5000 on your credit card and get it reduced to $2500, you should make sure that you can leave a balance of $1250 or less. If you owe $4000 and have no way of repaying it, getting your credit limit reduced can hurt you. On the other hand, if you need to get a larger loan and can pay off your credit card in full and reduce your limit to $2500, you may be able to improve your credit score in this way.

2) You have lots of credit. If you have several types of debts and credit accounts - lines of credit, credit cards, store charge cards, a mortgage, a car loan, and a personal line of credit - you may be close to overextending your credit, especially if each of these accounts is relatively large. You can't always close your accounts - especially if you are still paying your debts off - but reducing the limit may make you eligible for a loan should you need it.

3) You have some credit, but you don't want to close your accounts entirely because you have not had credit for very long. Sometimes, if you have several types of credit, it is not wise to close them, even if you can, since lenders like to see long-term relationships with lenders. Reducing the limits can make monthly payments more affordable and can give you a more significant credit boost than closing long-standing credit accounts.

4) You will not be taking out a loan very soon. In the short term, reducing your credit limits may lower your credit rating because your balances will make up a larger portion of a smaller credit, but in the long run, smaller charge accounts will boost your credit score by making repayment

of loans easier and by making you further from overextending your credit.

Start Repairing Your Credit Right Away After A Big Financial Upset

A big financial problem is an emotional as well as a monetary burden. Plenty of debtors feel so terrible about their financial problems and so uncertain about their money that they go into deep denial, refusing to think or work on their financial problems. This is likely to only make the problem worse.

Everybody suffers from financial difficulties occasionally and every professional in the field of finance - from loan managers to bankers - knows this. Plus, financial professionals - including lenders - want your business and so are willing to work with you to help you solve your problems.

If you have had a financial problem, or are even headed towards one, start working on repairing the situation right away. If your credit is suffering because you have not paid some bills, for example, don't make it worse by waiting until you are reported to a collection agency (by which time your credit rating will have taken an even worse hit). Instead, work on paying off your bills or arranging a payment schedule right away.

Consider Co-Signing for Loans - But Consider Well Before Taking the Leap.

If you have very poor credit scores following a bankruptcy or other disaster but need to get a loan, consider getting a co-signer. If your co-signer has assets or a better credit record, you may qualify for a better loan rate.

However, be wary - if your co-signer refuses to make payments, then both of you will suffer the credit fallout. Co-signers share responsibility for loans and credit - both of you will have worse credit scores if one of you does not pay.

On the other hand, if your cosigner has good credit and makes payments, then the co-signed loan can boost your credit score.

Don't Overlook Bankruptcy

A bankruptcy will affect your credit score more than just about anything. Worse, it will affect it for many years. In the first few years after a bankruptcy, you may not be able to get loans at all.

In short, a bankruptcy is a legal proceeding that either forgives you of your debts or allows you to pay off just a small fraction of your debt. It will nearly ruin your credit rating at first, but it will also allow you to dig out from overwhelming debt and reestablish an excellent credit rating again after years. A bankruptcy will no longer show up on your credit report after ten years.

If you are very seriously in debt and have no way of repaying your bills, a bankruptcy can help you by stopping collection call agencies and other problems. Also, if you have been very negligent in paying your large debts, your credit rating has already likely suffered greatly.

While a bankruptcy will depress it even further, at least it will give you the chance to repair your credit by giving you a "clean slate" free from large debts.

Don't Choose Bankruptcy as An Easy Out

Bankruptcy is a serious credit problem - it is not just a "ding" on your credit report - it is a huge red flag to lenders. After a bankruptcy, you will be ineligible for credit cards, many types of credit and will even be told what you can and cannot buy. The procedure of bankruptcy can also be draining. Bankruptcy should only be chosen as the last option if you really require your debts to be forgiven because you have no way of repaying them.

Learn from Your Mistakes

Everyone makes some credit mistakes sooner or later - it is very rare for someone to go through their entire lives without at least a few dings on their credit risk record. Don't beat yourself up over your mistakes - even if they are large ones. Instead, learn from your mistakes by analyzing them. Think of your credit mistakes as clues which can help you in the future to avoid the same problems:

-Do you develop credit problems because you overspend while shopping?

-Are you so disorganized that you forget to pay bills?

-Are your bills simply too large for your current income?

-Do you routinely get overcharged for things and fail to notice until much later?

Knowing what your mistakes are and finding solutions to the problems can go a long way towards helping you develop an excellent credit risk rating.

Chapter 7

Professional Help

Credit repair is big business, and there are many companies that will promise to help you get out of bad credit problems. There are some legitimate resources that can help you in improving your credit score, but there are also some less than reputable companies out there that will take your money but offer you few (if any) valuable services. A few basic tips will help you see the difference:

Seek Professional Help

If you are in over your head, and your credit is so bad that you cannot get a loan and may even be facing bankruptcy, you may want to seek help from professionals. There are some financial professionals that can help you with credit repair:

Bankruptcy Lawyers and Bankruptcy Advisors
Bankruptcy lawyers can help represent you in bankruptcy proceedings. Advisors can help you decide whether to

apply for a bankruptcy and how to proceed once you do decide to file.

While getting a bankruptcy lawyer and filing for bankruptcy can be upsetting and can dramatically affect your credit score for many years, it can also give you a chance to start over financially and can help you reestablish good credit again in the long run.

<u>Credit repair companies and credit counseling companies:</u> These companies can help you by acting on your behalf with credit companies, by advising you on what you can do to repay your bills faster, and by helping you make better financial decisions.

<u>Accountants and tax services:</u> Accountants and tax filing services can help you make the most of your money by making sure that you do not end up overspending on taxes.

<u>Bankers and bank officers:</u> Most banks today want to not only help you keep your money but are willing to work with you to make the most of it. As a banking service, many banks today offer free investing advice, saving

advice, and personalized meetings with bank officers that can help you figure out your money situation.

Lenders and bad credit lenders: How you deal with lenders will determine how well your credit score works. Avoiding too many inquiries by not applying for too many loans, establishing long-term business relationships with bankers, and doing business with bankers in an organized and professional way (i.e. paying your debts on time) will go a long way towards giving you a credit rating. In turn, an excellent credit rating will make it easier to deal with lenders.

Look Out for Credit Repair Companies

Many companies out there advertise that they can help you with credit repair, but the quality of these services - not to mention what they offer - varies widely. Some companies really can help you with credit repair while others are under investigation for suspect business practices. If you decide to seek help from a credit repair company, be sure that the company is legitimate and offers you viable services.

Check to make sure that the company has good standing with the Better Business Bureau and clients who are happy with the credit repair services they received from the company. Always read the paperwork carefully before you sign and make sure that you understand how much you are paying for and how much you are paying.

Before deciding to seek help from a credit help or credit counseling service, be sure that the problem cannot be resolved on your own. Indications that you may need credit counseling include:

-You cannot pay your bills and avoid the necessities of life.

-You avoid the phone, the mail, and the door because you are being harassed by collection agencies.

-You have avoided going out because you feel terrible about your financial state.

-You have no idea how you will repay your bills and loans -

you do not know where to start.

In addition, these companies tend to be more legitimate than credit repair companies that take your money, anyway.

It Will Be Easier for Financial Experts To Help You If You Seek Credit Repair Help Sooner Rather Than Later

If you do decide to seek credit repair help from the experts, it makes sense to seek that help before your financial situation spirals too far out of control. After all, credit repair experts can do little for you if your credit and financial situation are so bad that the only option left to you is bankruptcy.

Look Out for Credit Repair Scams

There are many credit repair scams out there. These scams often promise to help free you of bad credit, when the "experts" offering these services will either overcharge you, involve you in illegal activity, or put you in a worse financial situation. Look out for these most common scams:

1) Credit repair companies that tell you to lie on loan applications or suggest that you develop a second identity. This is illegal and dishonest. If a company suggests that you open accounts in a new name or falsify your information on loan applications, run, don't walk away.

You can be charged with fraud for doing this - and you will be held responsible for your actions, even if you were acting under the company's advisement. You certainly don't want to add legal troubles to your credit woes.

3) Credit repair companies that promise to pay your creditors from the money you pay to them and which they keep in an escrow account. This is a common scam, and it presents a huge problem for the debtor.

Here's how it works: the debtor gives money to the credit repair company, presumably for paying off debts. The company places the money in an escrow account where it grows. The idea is that the company will eventually pay off your debts when the amount reached in the account matches the debts. The problem is that in the meantime, the credit repair company is removing some money from the account for administrative fees while creditors are becoming more and more anxious, increasing the interest on the debts and even starting legal action against the debtor. This type of "credit help" can ruin your credit rating!

4) Credit repair companies that pressure you don't listen to you or want you to sign a contract you have not read. Such companies are not to be trusted and should be left well enough alone.

5) Companies that offer you fast or instant credit repair - no matter how bad your credit. This is simply a misleading claim that no company can legitimately deliver on. If you have terrible credit, it may take years to fully repair.

In many cases, these companies will claim that they can remove your poor credit history from your credit report by disputing it. This is false information. You simply cannot remove true and accurate information from your credit report. It is true that a credit bureau must investigate a claim of inaccurate information within thirty days, but this does not mean that the company will automatically remove the information.

In fact, if the information is accurate, the data will stand. Credit bureaus are aware of this common credit repair scheme and have become very good at detecting it. Many credit repair companies (and even some individuals) will try to dispute every ding on a credit report, hoping that the backlog of disputes will cause the credit bureau to automatically remove the offending items from the report (the credit bureau is legally required to remove disputed items it has not investigated within 30 days). This technique is a scam and is dishonest since you are not disputing inaccurate information.

Refuse to do business with credit help companies that use this practice.

6) Companies that don't tell you your rights or try to take money for things you could do yourself. You can get copies of your own credit reports and have the errors on

them fixed for free yourself - a company that does not tell you can do this yourself is taking money from you for things you can easily do yourself.

It is a dishonest practice, and companies who follow such business practices should be avoided at all costs. Also, if a company does not advise you of your credit rights, then that is an indication that they are not really on your side in the first place. Why would you want to do business with a company that does not help you?

Get A Good Team on Your Side To Help You With Your Credit Score

A good team of professionals can help you get your credit score back in shape. Your most important member of your team is yourself - you are the one with the financial agency and (with this book) the knowledge to become your own best advocate in credit repair. Besides this, you may want to check with your local library for financial help books. You may also want to include financial experts such as credit counselors or others to help you. If you decide to seek a team of experts to help, be sure that you check each person's credential, standing with the Better Business Bureau, and past clients to make sure that the person or company can really help you. Beyond this, make sure that you sign a contract or agreement with each professional member of your team.

Your Bank Has Good and Reliable Credit Information

One free and professional source of credit information is your bank. Your banking officer may be able to offer you a great deal of professional, free advice, especially as banks are trying harder and harder to provide excellent personal services to customers.

Your bank may also have many credit solutions - such as overdraft protection - that can help you keep your credit in good repair. Banks are realizing more and more that many of their clients are dealing with less than ideal credit. Banks are trying to meet the demands of this new group and can be a powerful ally for those who are trying to improve their credit.

Chapter 8

Good Financial Habits

Your credit score in some ways is meant to be a snapshot of your overall financial habits - especially your habits surrounding debts and other financial responsibilities. Developing some good financial habits can help your credit score by putting you in an excellent financial position.

Good financial habits will ensure that you don't get into too much debt and that you are able to meet your financial duties easily. There are a few financial habits that are especially credit-friendly:

Learn to Budget

One of the biggest reasons that people develop poor credit is overspending. In many cases, this overspending is caused by a lack of budget. A budget can tell you how much you should be spending on each item in your life. This allows your financial life to stay nicely organized.

Contrary to popular belief, a budget does not have to be constricting or boring or complicated. Simply note how much you earn each month, and on a piece of paper, write down how much you really need to spend on savings, rent, utilities, food, personal care, transportation, spending money, entertainment, hobbies, education, and other items. Make sure that your account for every expense.

Then, simply commit yourself to spending that amount on each item on your list. Of course, some expenses on your list will change each month - you may spend more on heating bills in the winter than in the summer, for example - but estimating can help ensure that you can meet all your financial responsibilities.

Live Within Your Means

Many people believe that if they only had more money, they would not have to worry about credit. In fact, this is not true. Many people who have money - or at least have all the trappings of money, including cars and nice homes - in fact, have terrible credit.

The secret of this is that it is not your income that decides whether you are a good credit risk or a bad one but rather how you handle money. You could be earning $7 per hour and still pay your bills and meet your financial responsibilities - in which case you will have terrific credit.

You could also be earning $300 000 a year and be in terrible debt and financial shape due to unpaid bills and excessive debt. The best way to ensure that you have an excellent credit rating - no matter what your income - is to spend less than you earn. That means living below your means. If you have a very small income, you may need to live with roommates in order to keep costs down. If you have a medium-sized income, that may mean saving more and entertaining less.

You may be interested to note that your income is not a factor in determining your credit score. Although your past and current employers are listed on your credit report - and although lenders may be able to guess your financial status from your loan amounts - your income does not count.

This means that if you won the lottery today or suddenly

inherited a large sum, your credit score would not increase. With your credit rating, what matters is how you manage your money, not how much you make.

Get Out of The Spending Habit

We are surrounded by advertisements that tell us to buy, buy, buy. When we want to read a book, we buy it. When we want to go somewhere, we take a cab or drive rather than walking.

Stopping spending consciously can be hard, but heading to your local library, walking instead of taking a car, buying a used computer instead of a new one - all can help you spend less and save more. There are several ways you can save money and pay off your debts faster by spending less:

1) When you head out, carry a small amount of cash with you and leave your credit cards at home. That way, you will not be able to overspend.

2) Stop catalogs from arriving at your house or discard

them unread - advertisements and catalogues encourage you to spend and buy when you don't need to.

3) Do it yourself. Eat in rather than dining out. Dining at restaurants or getting food delivered is always more expensive than doing your own cooking. Also, do your own taxes rather than farming the job out to someone else. Wash your own car, run your own errands, mow your own lawn. When you do something yourself, you spend less.

4) Watch less television. It sounds strange, but television can make you overspend - television contains many professionally-created advertisements pushing us to spend and spend. These ads are so well done that not spending after watching them is sometimes very difficult (just what advertisers want!). Switching off your television can help you avoid temptation.

5) Make do or do without. While you are repairing your credit, channel all your extra money into paying off debts and reestablishing good credit. Make do with what you have and avoid shopping as much as possible.

6) Buy discount or used. Whether it is furniture or shoes, you can save money by refusing to pay retail price.

Saving your money by spending less can let you pay off your debts faster, something that can improve your credit score dramatically.

Save

One of the best ways to ensure that your credit rating stays good is to save money each month. Whether you are able to save $25 a month or $200 or even more, saving and investing your savings will prepare you for financial emergencies, will get you out of overspending, and will allow you to build investments that can help you in later years.

With savings at your bank, you don't have to worry that sudden illness will make you unable to pay your bills, resulting in dings on your credit.

Saving ten percent of your income is a nice, reasonable

goal. You can use your invested savings to make sure that your debts never get overwhelming. Most employers and banks will even deduct a certain amount of money from your paycheck or account each month to be put into investments.

This can be a very convenient way to save, as you are unlikely to miss or spend money you have taken out before you can get your hands on it.

Keep Track of Your Money

Most people are surprised by how quickly their money seems to be spent. This is because impulse spending and small-change spending really adds up. Small-change spending is small spending we do without even thinking about it - buying a coffee or a newspaper we don't need.

Impulse spending refers to simply buying things we don't use or need. In both cases, we end up spending too much unnecessarily, and this is a problem in credit repair because you want to be channeling as much money as you can into savings and debt repayment so that you can repair your credit.

For a month, try keeping a daily record of every penny you spend - including the money you spend on phones, the money you spend on tips, everything. You will be amazed where your money goes. Keeping track of your money this way does two things:

1) It automatically cuts down on spending. If you have to write down where you spend your money, you will be much more careful what you spend your money on.

2) It allows you to see where you waste your money and take steps to stop the bad habit. If you notice that you always buy the newspaper on Saturday but never read it, for example, you can stop buying the paper on that day. Small savings can add up over the years and can put you in good financial shape which will be reflected in your credit risk rating.

Take Out One Pleasure and Save It Up

-Do you have cable?

-Do you subscribe to lots of magazines?

-Do you build your DVD collection so fast that you can't even watch all the movies you collect?

We all entertain ourselves with money, but most of us have at least one or two entertainments that we have either outgrown or don't enjoy as much as we once did. Cutting that expense out and investing the savings can put us well on our way to saving for retirement or paying off our bills. If you give up your cable television, for example, you can pay off your credit cards that much faster, improving your credit score.

Build Assets and Capital

Whether it is buying a car, a home, or creating an investment portfolio, having assets can help improve your credit score by allowing you take out secured credit or credit in which your assets are used as collateral. When you take out secured credit (such as a mortgage), you enjoy lower interest rates and easier approval. As you repay your secured debt, your credit score will improve.

Even better, lenders do look at the types of credit you have. If you have a mix of secured and unsecured credit, you will enjoy better risk rating scores as it will indicate that you have the means to repay your debts.

Building assets and capital is also a way of building financial stability which can help protect your credit score. If you have assets such as savings or investments, then you have a way of generating income or repaying debts in case of an emergency. You also have ready money you can use in case of unexpected medical bills or other problems.

Find More Ways to Income

While you are repairing your credit, you will want to channel as much money as you can into savings and debt repayment. For this, having a second income or even just a few hundred dollars a month more can mean that you get your credit into shape faster.

Having a secondary form of income can also keep your credit safe - if you lose your job, you can use the money you make from a secondary source to repay your bills until you find another form of employment.

There are many ways to get more income:

-You can ask your employer for a raise.
-You can start to sell something through the Internet or a company.
-You can establish your own small business that can be tended to on the side.
-You can rent out part of your home to make some extra money.
-You can get a part-time or weekend job.

Whatever you do, finding an alternate source of income can help your credit immensely.

Prepare for Financial Emergencies

Few of us think about what would happen if we lost our jobs or suddenly became too ill to work. The thought is simply too terrible to contemplate in many cases, especially if we are living from paycheck to paycheck with a job as it is.

The fact is, though, that financial emergencies happen to almost everyone at some point and they can have a devastating impact on your credit. In fact, most people who declare bankruptcy do so because of a huge financial disaster such as sudden unemployment, substantial medical bills, a lawsuit, or divorce. Despite this, few people plan for these problems, even though they can happen to anyone.

If you want to keep your credit score in good trim, you should know exactly what you would do in case of an emergency. Developing an actual written plan can help you by letting you take action to save your credit as soon as an emergency occurs. Some items that could be on your financial emergency plan could include:

1) A list of all assets you could liquidate if you had to.

2) A list of all extras or luxuries you could cut out of your life right away if there were a problem (i.e. newspaper subscriptions, cable television, water delivery service,

Friday nights at the movies).

3) A list of any resources you have that could help you in case of an emergency. Maybe you know a lawyer who deals in financial facets of the law. Maybe you have insurance that could help you. Perhaps your employer offers a severance package. Whatever it is, write it down. Keeping a list of these resources will make them easier to access in case of an emergency.

4) Other ways you could get money if you had to - jobs you could take, things you could rent out to others.

Get Overdraft Protection, Insurance on Your Credit Cards Or Other Services To Keep Your Credit In Good Shape

Talk to your bank and lenders about services they offer to keep you safe. Overdraft protection, for example, is a necessary service that often costs nothing or very little extra but which protects you in case you withdraw too much money from your bank account.

With overdraft protection, you do not get a "ding" on your credit report or a charge for insufficient funds. In most cases, you get a day or two to add more money to the account to cover the gap. Some credit cards and other loans offer a similar service or offer insurance which protects you in case you lose your job and are unable to pay for a few months.

Get Insurance

Insurance for health, your car, your home, and for liability can help you avoid the huge legal and medical bills that can occur from an accident or sudden problem. For a small monthly fee, you are covered against unexpected events that can drain your finances and leave you with out-of-control debt.

Get A Prenuptial Agreement And Have A Lawyer Go Over All Your Business Contracts

Most bankruptcies are caused by the fallout that occurs as a result of business failures, lawsuits, health costs, and divorces. Getting a prenuptial agreement helps to ensure that a divorce will not adversely affect your finances and lead to a ruined credit rating (keeping accounts separate while married is also a good idea, as your spouse's own financial troubles can all too easily become your own). Having a lawyer look over contracts can at least reduce the risks of unfavorable agreements that can put you at a disadvantage in business.

Chapter 9

How To Think Like a Lender

If you think like a lender, you can see which habits and traits you need to develop in order to be considered a good credit risk. Thinking like a lender will help you understand how you must manage your money to be appealing to lenders. There are few tips that can put you into the right mindset:

Know How Money Works

Reading books about money and understanding how your accounts and loans work can go a long way towards helping you keep your credit in good repair. For example, if you know that some loans will charge you extra if you pay off your loan faster while others will not, you will be in a better position to make financial decisions.

Plus, the more you know about money in general, the more comfortable you will feel with it and the better decisions you will be able to make, which will help improve your overall financial state and will help you keep your credit in good shape.

You don't need to do heavy-duty research to appreciate how money works. One easy way to consider money is to think of it the way you think of time. You likely hate to waste time, and you want to make the best use of it possible. Apply the same attitudes to your financial life and watch your finances soar!

If overspending has caused you to have a bad credit score, consider the following sneaky mindset trick: equate your money with your time. For example, if you make twenty dollars an hour, then a magazine subscription of $20 will represent one hour of your work.

Imagine an hour of your work and ask yourself whether the subscription is worth the time you put into the twenty dollars. Once you start seeing money as something that comes from your hard work rather than a general "thing" impulse spending will seem much less attractive, and it will be easier to keep your credit card limits low, and your bank account stocked up with cash!

Take Care of Those Things Besides A Credit Score That Affects How Lenders View You

Lenders will often look at not only your credit score but at other financial indicators, such as your income, employment record, and savings. Keeping these things in order can complement your credit score and can help you get good overall credit. Some lenders have their own ways of calculating credit scores, so keeping your overall financial system in good shape is one way to ensure that you are in good shape in all lenders' eyes.

Be aware that when lender asks to see your credit score, the credit bureaus send not only your credit score but also the top four reasons why your credit score is lowered. The most common reasons for lowered credit scores are:

1) Serious delinquency in repaying accounts or bills.

2) Public record of bankruptcy, civil judgment, or report to a collection agency.

3) Recent unpaid or late paid debts or accounts.

4) Short-term credit record.

5) Lots of new accounts.

6) Many accounts have late payments, defaults, or non-payments.

7) Large debts or amounts owed.

Knowing that your lender sees these possible problems can help you see the need to develop the best possible face to present to a lender. Lenders who look at your entire credit report may get a more positive picture of you than lenders who see only a number and four reasons for a lower score.

Follow Up On Closed Accounts

You closed a store card years ago - but is it still listed as an open account? Bureaucratic mix-ups happen, often quite frequently. If you want to keep your credit score reasonable, you need to follow up on financial details.

Whenever you close an account - whether it's a credit account, bank account, or utility company account, make sure that you get written confirmation that the account is closed and paid in full and then follow up a few months later with the company to confirm the closed account. This simple precaution can save you hours of frustration - not to mention a lowered credit score.

Don't Move Around A Lot

Lenders like to see stability - it suggests stability in financial matters as well as in your life, and makes you a better credit risk. Plus, every time you move, you may have to change your credit information - including switching banks. This negatively affects your credit score by not allowing you to develop long-term relationships with lenders.

Remember: Your current and past addresses are listed on your credit report even if they do not directly affect your credit score. Any lender looking at your full credit report will be pleased to see that you create a stable life for yourself. Not moving too frequently can also save you money on moving costs, which can add up quite quickly.

Don't Change Jobs Frequently

Of course, there will be times when you will have to change jobs. However, avoiding changing jobs unnecessarily will help improve your credit score by allowing you to stay in one place and build a steady financial situation.

Your credit report also shows your current and past jobs - if a lender sees that you change jobs frequently, he or she may wonder whether you have the life stability required to handle debt responsibilities. Also, the lender cannot see why you left a job. If there are many employers listed on your credit report, the lender may wonder whether you have not been fired from jobs and whether that is an indication that you will be unable to pay your debts due to unemployment at some point in the future.

A lender makes their money by the interest charged on a loan. If you default on a loan, you cause the lender to lose money. Above all, the lender wants to see evidence on your credit record that you have the traits that will make you repay the loan - with interest.

Frequent job changes may indicate - to some lenders - that you will simply disappear with the money or default on a loan. Having a stable life - including a longer-term job and one place of residence - may indicate to lenders, on the other hand, that you are building up roots in a place and so will be unlikely to move and default.

Avoid Changing Switching Credit Companies And Credit Accounts A Lot

Credit companies will often offer you special introductory rates, generous free gifts or other incentives to switch companies. However, you should resist the temptation unless you have a reasonable reason to switch. Establishing a good credit relationship with one company - having one credit card from your college days, for example - is a good way to show lenders that you are a steady sort of person who is likely to take money matters seriously. That is exactly what lenders want to see. Switching accounts and lenders make you appear fickle and less than reliable.

Keep Your Records Up To Date

Not knowing what is going on in your own financial life is courting disaster. Keep one file folder in your home which contains your financial information - and review this periodically. If something changes in your life - you get married, you start a family, you move or change jobs, look through your financial folder and contact everyone who needs to be contacted to update them on the change. This will help make sure that all your creditors have the information they need about you. Keeping your own records up to date will help you make sure that everyone who handles your finances is also up-to-date.

Always Be Sure That Your Creditors Know Your Current Address

If you move and forget to inform all your creditors of your new address, you may not get all your bills, making you look like a deadbeat debtor and making your credit score plummet. Make sure that you either close your credit accounts or get your new address and contact information to your creditors.

When you move, make sure that you inform credit card companies, stores you have credit cards with, banks, credit unions, and anyone else you do financial business with. Better yet, also arrange with the post office to have your mail automatically forwarded to you at your new address. This will ensure that any creditors you may have overlooked will still be able to contact you - and you will have a second chance to remind them of your address change.

Talk To Lenders And Creditors

Many people are hesitant to keep an open line of communication with their lenders because they are embarrassed about their financial state or because they feel unsure about the position.

Lenders can't read your mind, though. They do not know that you can't make a payment this month but will be able to make a double payment next month because of a banking error. They simply see that you have failed to make a payment - this may indicate a temporary problem or a decision on your part to default on your loan.

Without your input, your creditors have no way of knowing, and since their profits and money are at risk, they tend to take the more conservative view and even assume the worst. Keeping the lines of communication open as soon as a problem develops can help reassure your lenders and can help your creditors see that you are responsible with their money.

Talking to lenders as soon as a problem develops can be an effective way to prevent a ding on your credit score that can affect your credit score. For example, if you are giving trouble paying your bills, you can often work out a more reasonable payment schedule.

In most cases, you will not get a ding on your credit record if you do this because the lender will have some assurance that your financial obligations will still be met. In fact, one of the things that most credit repair companies do is to arrange for more reasonable payment schedules. With a simple phone call, you can do this for yourself at no charge.

Lenders want, above all, to be repaid so that their interest rates can earn them a profit. By communicating whenever there is a problem and showing that you are willing to work hard to meet your responsibilities, you show your creditors that they will get their money and this makes lenders more willing to work with you to ensure that your credit rating is not severely affected by one missed or late payment. Speaking with your creditors can help establish a good working relationship that can help keep your credit rating in good shape.

Get Lenders To Waive Late Fees And Charges

If you have missed some payments or made some late payments, lenders will often charge you a fee for non-payment. This not only adds insult to injury - you have to pay more on your bills and get a ding on your credit - but also makes bills more challenging to repay since the bills are now higher. You can phone the lender and get the charge waived in most cases, though. This is a secret that credit repair companies have long known and is one of the first services they will perform on your behalf. You can easily accomplish this for yourself, however, at no cost.

Lenders want to get paid, and if they think that you will pay your bill more quickly by waiving the late fee, they will most often gladly remove the fee in exchange for prompt payment.

Chapter 10

Credit Repair Strategy

Staying organized and on-track is very important when you are trying to boost your credit score because there are so many details to follow up on and so many things to remember. A few basic organization tips can help make sure that you do not overlook anything that can cost you your good credit score:

Stay Financially Organized

Keep all your financial records - including tax records - in one place. Note the days you paid your bills on the bills themselves. Note how much you owe and where you owe money. Keeping your financial information in one place allows you to refer to it easily. Seeing all your financial life in one place also makes it easier for you to see where your credit and your financial life still needs work.

Some of the information you may want to keep in your financial file includes:

-Bills

-Tax receipts and forms

-Articles and pamphlets about debt

-Your credit reports and scores

-A list of contacts that affect your financial life (such as your bank and credit agencies, for example)

-Your written emergency plan, detailing what you should do in case of a sudden loss of job or other problem

-Banking information

-Financial forms

-Investment information

-Deeds to your assets (such as your house)

-Agreements you have signed for loans and other financial services

-A list of your financial goals

-Insurance forms

You may want to buy a box and keep your separate information in different labeled folders (tax information together, for example, and bills in another folder) for easy referencing. Whatever system you use, you will find it much easier to manage your finances - and your credit - if you don't have to hunt for random pieces of paper.

Set Short-Term Goals and Do Frequent Credit Self-Checks in Order To Track Your Progress

Credit repair takes time and effort. Some days, it will seem that you are getting no closer to a better credit score at all. In order to keep track of your progress and in order to keep going forward, you need to set goals and keep track of what you are doing.

For example, setting a goal such as "I will improve my credit score" is far too broad. Set smaller goals, such as "I will talk to my bank about budgeting this week" or "I will pay off half my credit card bill by next month." These goals work better because they are manageable and have a built-in deadline.

Writing your goals on a calendar or planner you look at every day will motivate you to keep working on your credit repair and will keep you making the small steps that can lead to better credit. If you review how far you have come each month or week, you can really keep track of your progress and see how much you still have to do.

Take Care of The Details When Applying For Credit Or For A Credit Report

Little things make a big difference. Misquoting your social insurance number or using a slightly different name (Jane Doe Smith instead of Jane Smith) can make a big difference since credit bureaus can count the two names as different people. Making sure that you fill out each financial form accurately and in the same way can go a long way in ensuring that there are no mistakes in identity that can affect your credit score.

Don't Make the Mistake Of Thinking That Small Differences In Credit Scores Or Loan Interest Rates Won't Make A Big Impact

A few points on a credit score can mean the difference

between a lender offering you a prime rate reserved for the best credit risks and the worse interest rate offered to less than prime customers. This may amount to only a few percentages in different loan rates, but this can make a huge impact, especially on a large purchase. For example, a few percentage points on a long-term fixed-rate loan can mean the difference between tens of thousands of dollars saved - or tens of thousands of dollars overspent.

It is in your best interest to boost your credit score by every percentage point you can and to fight for the very lowest interest rate loans you can. After all, if you have larger payments each month due to a higher interest rate than you deserve, it will be harder for you to repay your bills. Also, you will qualify for fewer loans if you have higher-than-needed interest rates, as you will be able to afford fewer of the larger monthly payments.

If You Need To Repair Your Credit, Stay Organized With A To-Do List That Ensures You Won't Forget Anything

As you can likely tell by now, credit repair is not one

magical solution but instead lots of relatively small things you can do to help repair your credit. To make sure that you don't overlook any one thing, you may want to develop a to-do list that you can post and check off.

You may list credit accounts you need to close, accounts you need to pay down, people you need to contact, and things you need to check out or research. As you tick off each item, you will get a real sense of accomplishment knowing that you are taking steps to improve your finances. Keeping a credit repair checklist posted will also keep you on track and let you know what you still need to do.

Automate Your Finances

Thanks to automatic bank payments, you can have your bills taken out of your checking account each month or even charged to your credit card. If you are the sort of person who gets dings on their credit report because you can never remember to pay your bills on time, this can be a beneficial service.

You can even set up your email service to send you automatic reminders of bills that are due soon so that you can pay them. This sort of automation is one of the more helpful things about high-tech living and can help you keep your credit score clean if your credit score suffers mainly from your own forgetfulness or disorganization.

Chapter 11

Your Credit Score and Loans

Loans affect your credit score more than almost any other item on your credit report. The types of loans you have, how long you have had loans, the amounts you owe and your payment history on your loans have one of the biggest impacts on your credit score. If you can control your loans, you can boost your credit score. There are a few tips that can get you well on your way to painlessly managing your loans:

Refinance Loans

If you got a poor deal on a loan - especially a major loan such as a car or home loan - or if your credit rating has improved since you got your loan, you may want to consider refinancing. Refinancing means that you take your loan to another lender in order to enjoy better terms or rates.

You don't want to do this too often - it prevents you from developing long-term relationships with lenders and results in inquiries on your credit report - but if you have good reasons to refinance, it can help you repay your debts. For example, if you can get more reasonable monthly bills that you will be able to repay, refinancing can help prevent all those non-payment credit dings that come from not being able to pay your bills. Making your payments more affordable can save you money and your credit score.

In the short term, refinancing can push your credit score down, as you will acquire inquiries on your credit report as you look for a new lender and as you close old accounts and open new accounts. In the long term, though, refinancing can be a good way of boosting your credit score. If you are now missing or delaying payments because you cannot afford monthly bills, for example, refinancing a loan or two can be a good way to get back on track and can get you repairing your credit score again.

Look for Loans That Are Offered for Bad Credit Risks

If your credit score is bad, but you need a loan, consider services that cater to people with poor credit scores. These companies know that some creditors with poor credit scores will still make their payments on time and so are willing to speak with debtors other companies would reject out of hand. You may have to deal with higher interest rates, but choosing a bad credit lender can go a long way to ensuring that your credit score won't disqualify you for a loan.

In the long run, you can always refinance your loan to take advantage of a better rate once your credit score improves.

Always Know Your Credit Score Before Speaking to Lenders

Many people assume that having an excellent credit score is enough when applying for a loan. It is not. Some lenders are not terribly scrupulous about offering you the best rate - especially if they can gain by having you pay higher interest. Some lenders will try to tell you that your credit score is lower than it is and that disqualifies you from a better rate. Some may rely on your ignorance (or what they think of your ignorance) about your credit score to quote you a worse rate.

Never let a lender do this. Always look up your credit score before shopping for a major loan and if you are quoted a rate you think is unfair, speak up and tell the credit officer that your credit score of 700 (or whatever the score is) seems to indicate a better loan.

Show the lender your printed copy of your credit score. If the lender tries to tell you that lenders get more accurate credit scores than customers who look up their own credit scores or tries to tell you that your credit score has changed, walk away. There are many reputable lenders out there. Find one of them rather than relying on a lender who will try to lie to make a profit.

Consider Speaking to Lenders Face-To-Face If You Have A Bad Credit Score

If you apply for a loan over the telephone or online, your credit score will count the most, because that is all the lender will likely look at before getting back to you with a quote. If you have bad credit but still need a loan, meeting with a lender face to face is your best bet because an actual meeting allows a lender to get an impression of you, and allows you to explain the problems you have had in the past and the things you are doing now to make yourself a better credit risk.

When you meet worth a lender in person, you force them to stop looking at you as a credit score number and make them look at you as an entire person. This can be a huge advantage for you (especially if you are personable) and can help you get the loan your credit score does not completely qualify you for.

Chapter 12

Make It Easier on Yourself

Credit repair is no picnic. It requires continual work and effort to get a good credit score and to improve a bad one. In today's busy life, you stand a much better chance of getting a better credit score if you make it as easy on yourself as possible. In many cases, people have low credit scores, not because of carelessness or indifference, but because hectic lifestyles lead to oversights and missed credit payments. There are several things you can do to make good credit almost automatic:

Don't Let a Bad Credit Score Make You Swear Off Purchases You Must Make

You will make life much harder for yourself if you deny yourself things you need - such as medical treatments - because your credit is poor. If you have bad credit but need money for something urgent, consider a secured loan or a bad credit loan with generous terms. Do not let bad credit affect your ability to stay safe and healthy.

Some people think that getting credit while trying to repair their FICO score is bad idea. While it is true that you may not get the best interest rates on the loans you get in the time before your credit score is improved, getting loans that you need may simply be too important to put off.

Make Arrangements to Pay Your Bills When You Are On Vacation Or Ill

When we go on vacation, of course we want to get away from it all, but when we forget to pay our bills while away, we risk getting dings on our credit that can affect our credit risk rating.

Make it part of your vacation practice to pay bills in advance or to arrange someone to pay your bills while you are away. Similarly, while you are ill, arrange to have bills paid so that bills don't pile up and so that you don't get marked as a "non-payer." It is frustrating to be trying to improve a credit score only to suffer a setback over a small oversight.

Consider Online Banking or Telephone Banking To Make Bill Payment Easier

If you have trouble getting your payments in on time, consider online or telephone banking. This simple system is now available from virtually every bank and can help you pay your bills in minutes - at any time of the day or night. If you travel a lot, online or telephone banking can be a real life-saver as it will allow you to pay your bills no matter where you are.

Plus, you get instant confirmation of the paid bill, and your payment is counted instantly. You no longer have to worry about payments getting lost in the mail or getting lost in a bureaucratic shuffle - the record of the payment is right on your bank account statement.

If you lead a busy lifestyle and have several late payments of bills simply because you can't quite keep up with the errand of paying bills, online or telephone banking can be the solution that can help your credit rating by effectively putting a stop to late or unpaid bills. With these two very convenient and quick payment options, there really is no excuse for unpaid accounts.

Simplify Your Bills

You can often get great discounts by choosing to get several services from the same company - for example, a package deal from your phone company can give you internet access, long distance phone plans, and cable television - all on one bill and all in one low price. Pooling your insurance into one package from one insurance provider can have the same effect. Reducing the number of bills you get can make it easier for you to pay your bills and so reduces the chances that your credit rating will be affected by non-paid or late paid bills.

Pay Your Bills as Soon As You Get Them

If you leave your bills until later, you may forget and end up being listed as a late payer. Some companies may not report you to credit bureaus right away, but others report even one skipped or late payment, which can show up on your credit report and affect your credit rating.

Set Aside a Regular Day, Time, And Place For Paying Bills

If you are too busy to pay your bills as they arrive, set aside one hour each week for paying your bills and ordering your finances. Have the same place and time set aside each week, so that paying incoming bills and taking care of your finances becomes an automatic good habit.

Make sure that the place you set aside is quiet and contain everything you need - including pens, a calendar, stamps, envelopes, and your payment information. Making bill paying automatic in this way can reduce the number of non-payments and late payments you make on your bills, and reducing these problems can help improve your credit risk rating.

Record Your Financial Duties on A Calendar - Just Like All Your Other Appointments

If you mark down when bills are due, when you need to make payments, and what you need to accomplish to boost your credit score in a visible place you check often, you are less likely to overlook important appointments and deadlines.

Go Online

There are a number of online resources that can help you find credit information and can help you with your credit repair project:

The FICO website - www.myfico.com - contains lots of useful credit repair information and even allows you to order credit reports and scores.
The credit bureaus (transunion.com, equifax.com, and experian.com) allow you to order credit scores and credit reports online.

Through these online sites, you can also get information on reporting errors on your credit report. Your bank likely offers online banking as well, which can make managing your accounts easier and simpler for you each month.

Most companies - including utility companies and credit card companies - will now allow you to get your bills right in your inbox. This is a very handy feature as it allows you to get your bill right away, it cuts down on the amount of mail you get, and allows you to get and pay your bill online through online banking. Plus, many accounting software packages now allow you to coordinate all your financial information through one program, which can make taking care of your finances much more automatic and timely.

Chapter 13

Student Credit Repair

Students are increasingly worried about credit and credit scores - and for a good reason. Student debts are rising, and the numbers of students who leave school with ruined credit scores are rising as well. Many experts blame larger credit card debts and rising tuition costs (that lead to larger student loans).

Despite the pressures of today's student life, though, it is possible to leave school with a good credit score and in fact to develop good financial habits that can lead to a lifetime of good credit ratings. There are a few tips that can make the college years a credit-booster instead of a credit disaster:

If You Are A Student, You Have A Great Secret Weapon For Credit Repair And Credit Help - Your School's Financial Aid Office

If you are a college student, your school's financial aid

office should be one of your first stops at the campus. Few students visit this office regularly while they are in school, and this is a mistake. The financial aid office at most universities and colleges has more than enough information to help you keep your credit score in tip-top shape.

The financial aid office offers one-on-one financial counseling, information about scholarships, tips on budgeting, books on money, and many more resources. The officers at your university or college financial aid office can offer you help on almost any aspect of financial help - including helping you figure out credit scoring. Plus, many financial aid offices have workshops that can teach you about dealing with money and credit, and even offer free tax filing services, services that are extremely useful.

In fact, the financial aid offices at most colleges and universities are so useful that you may want to call the school you attended in the past to ask whether alumni are eligible for any services at the financial aid office. The resources that you a get for free from these offices are simply too good to miss.

If You Are A Student (And Especially A Student With Student Loans), Budget Carefully

Student loans need to be paid back and are more and more often in large amounts. Taking out the smallest loans you can and sticking to a budget can help establish good credit habits that can help ensure that you have a good credit score when you leave university. Plus, since student loans are for a limited amount, you can efficiently budget because you will know exactly how much money you will make each month and how much money you will be spending on student housing, tuition, and other expenses.

Try to Pay For Education Through Means Other Than Loans

Student loans are becoming a problem for more and more students. On the one hand, student and college loans can help students who could otherwise not afford go to college or university.

On the other hand, though, huge student loans can be a terrible financial burden after graduation.

While it is true that most college and student loans do not have to be repaid until after graduation, the time after graduation usually carries some large financial responsibilities. Many college graduates want or need a car, a good job, and possibly a house or home. Each of these things requires a good credit standing, but too large student loans not only require larger monthly repayments but also may affect credit scores by overextending credit.

As tuition fees rise, larger student loans are becoming the norm, leading to financial hardship down the road for many students. To avoid this, you should take out the smallest loan you can, relying on jobs, savings, scholarships, bursaries, and other forms of financial aid to make up the rest of your tuition and living expenses. You should rely on loans as a last - not a first - alternative.

Student and college loans are an investment in your future since they can help you get the education you need in order to get a great and fulfilling career. However, these loans are a serious and usually long-term financial responsibility. They should not be undertaken lightly. If you need a loan to pay for college, you should get the smallest loan you can and should get the best terms and rates on it possible. In general, need-based government-subsidized student loans generally offer the best terms and rates. After that, college and student loans from private lenders may offer decent rates. Personal loans and credit cards should only be used when absolutely necessary to pay for an education, as these tend to have higher interest rates and require that you start repaying them right away.

(Almost) Never Default on A Student Loan

Many students think that defaulting on a student loan after graduation is a smart way to get rid of a debt. After all, they no longer need the money for school and in fact I need the money for settling into a job and new home.

However, defaulting on a student loan is a terrible mistake in almost all cases, because it affects your credit rating very negatively. If you have student loans, it is important that you start repaying them on schedule and that you repay them on time. Doing so will improve your credit score.

If you are having trouble repaying your student and college loans, speak to the lenders rather than ignoring the problem. Most lenders will give you a six-month grace period after graduation so that you can find a job and settle into post-college life before repaying your loans.

If you have several loans, your lenders may be willing to help you pool them into one larger loan payment that requires smaller monthly payments. Some lenders will also give a few months grace in case of unemployment.

Read your loan agreements carefully to find out what your student loans are like and what is forgiven in them. If you need to, work out a different payment schedule, seek out refinancing, or find some other way to repay.

Only default on your student loans as a last resort when you really have no way of repaying your debts. In that finality, be prepared for the decision to affect your credit score quote badly for some time.

Once you default on one loan, it really counts against your credit rating - especially since as a new graduate you do not have a long credit history yet. After all, lenders who see that you have defaulted on one financial responsibility will wonder why you wouldn't default on their loan, as well. After defaulting on your student loan, you may be unable to get credit for some time, and you will have to work much, much harder to re-establish good credit.

Save Money by Taking Advantage Of Student Discounts Or Student Life

One of the advantages of student life is that it is inexpensive. Student housing or rooms rented with roommates create inexpensive living, on-campus facilities offer great services at discount rates, and many businesses offer student-only deals.

Try to take advantage of these offers to make your student money stretch further so that you have taken out the smallest student loans possible. Look around to find the best student-deal offers, ranging from travel deals to free tax filing services, available from your campus and surrounding businesses.

Make use of the free services on campus - such as renting movies for free from the film department or working out in the school gym - rather than paying for these same services outside the campus.

Follow The "Cash for Wants, Loans For Needs" Rule

Many students fall in love with their credit cards. Credit card companies know this, too, and routinely heavily advertise on college campuses, even offering students free food or gifts to fill out a credit application. While the convenience of credit cards is tempting, it is a good habit to use credit cards only for major purchases, saving cash for entertainment, food, clothes, and other like items. This is because studies have repeatedly shown that those who pay cash for items routinely spend less than those charging or using debit cards to pay.

Using only cash for entertainment and other small needs ensures you won't spend more than you have to and also ensures that you won't be paying for months for something that is long gone.

Make Learning About Money a Priority

Whether you attend information sessions at the financial aid office, read about money in books, or meet with your bank's financial officers, learning how to manage your money is an important part of school life.

For many students, their time away from home is one of the first times they are responsible for finances - including bills. Learning to handle this responsibility well early on in life ensures that you will enjoy a good credit standing your whole life. Learning about money will also help you prevent costly credit mistakes.

Start Building Credit Early - And Do It Well

Start building credit early - even before college starts, if you plan on taking out college loans. Ask your parents to sign over a bill that you pay on time each month. Get a credit card with a low limit and a bank account that you balance each month. Avoid opening several charge cards at once - not only will they be hard to repay, but having several new accounts when you have a short credit history will cause your credit rating to drop. Get a part-time job.

Each of these things can help you establish good credit, high in turn can help you get a reasonable student loan rate. More importantly, establishing credit early will help ensure that you have a long (and good) credit history by the time you graduate from college, which will help you with all your important, large post-graduation expenses.

Chapter 14

Dealing with Your Debt

Debt is a major factor in your credit score. If you have too much of it (or none at all) or if you have trouble repaying your debts on time, your credit score will plummet. Keeping your debts reasonable and paid, on the other hand, will do more than almost anything else to improve your credit score. Here are a few tips that can ensure that your debts help you boost your credit score:

Consolidate Your Loans to Make Repaying Them Easier

Having lots of loans and debt is one of the biggest reasons leading to poor credit ratings. The larger your debts, the worse your credit rating and the more likely that you will find yourself with large monthly bills that are difficult to repay.

Consolidating your loans means that you take out one large

loan to repay all your creditors so that you only have one large loan to repay. While the overall amount of the loan does not change - if you owed $20 000 to five different companies, you will still owe $20 000 but to only one lender - but the interest rates and monthly payments are usually quite smaller, and this can help meeting your debt obligations much easier.

Debt consolidation can be an especially good idea if you have lots of high-interest debt and lots of bills that are hard to keep track of. One smaller monthly payment will be easier to remember and will help make bill time less painful.

Pay Down Your Debts by Making Larger Than Minimal Payments

If you only pay down the minimum amount on each of your loans, it will take you a long, long time to pay down your loans. This is because most lenders only require that you pay down slightly more than the interest amount on your debt each month. Even a debt of a few hundred dollars could take several years to repay this way.

Paying down your debts by putting down more than the minimum required monthly payment can help you pay down your debts faster and so can boost your credit score. Paying down more than you need to also shows lenders that you are in good financial shape and conscientious about your debts - two qualities that definitely make you an attractive credit risk to lenders.

If You Are Taking Out a New Loan, Consider Putting Down A Larger Down Payment To Take Out A Smaller Loan

Doing all you can to take out a smaller loan - by putting down a larger down payment or buying a less expensive car or home (if that is what the loan is for), for example - can help ensure that you don't overextend your credit and can help ensure that your monthly payments on the debt will be reasonable and affordable to you.

In fact, for larger purchases, some debtors take out piggyback loans, most often for a mortgage. They borrow money for a down payment so that they can get a better rate deal on the larger second loan they take out to pay for the purchase.

Do your math before making a big purchase - you may find that a larger down payment - even if you have to borrow to get it - can help your credit by making your payments more affordable and by ensuring that you don't overextend your credit.

Use Loan Calculators to Estimate Your Finances and Keep Your Credit Rating In Good Shape

Online loan calculators are a useful tool that can help you determine how much of an interest rate you should pay, how much in monthly payments you can afford, and how much your loan will cost you in interest over the long term.

Online loan calculators are free to use and can help you figure out how to make your debts more affordable. There are online loan calculators for auto loans, home loans, and personal loans. If you are going to be getting a new loan, these calculators can be a powerful resource.

Avoid Payday Loans

Payday loans are also called "cash advance loans," and they are small and short-term loans that carry a very high-interest rate. Some companies have even begun to advertise them as loans to help you repair your credit, but this is very misleading. Some companies suggest that these loans can help you pay off your bills and so establish good credit, but if you cannot afford to pay your payday loans on time, you must "roll-over" or extend the loan - often at huge expense and interest. Many people get into a payday loans cycle, whereby much of their monthly paycheck goes towards paying off their ever-growing payday loans.

In fact, several states are investigating payday loans for possible illegal activity stemming from usury laws. If you cannot afford your bills one month, you are much better off trying to arrange an alternate schedule of payment with the companies you owe money to rather than risking your credit rating through payday loans. Payday loans may be excellent in a real emergency, but the payday loans cycle gets very unaffordable very fast and can ruin your credit rating.

Do Not Use One Debt to Repay Another

This results in accumulating interest and so increasingly unpayable bills. If you use one credit card to pay off another, for example, you are paying interest on interest, and paying off the new credit card bill will be more difficult.

This method will also mean that you will always be looking for new credit and new debt to pay off your increasing debts. It makes more sense to get a second job or arrange for a new payment schedule.

Paying off your debts with another debt may help you in the short run - you will not have a late payment on your credit record - but in the long run the larger debt load will make maintaining good credit more and more difficult. The only exception to this rule is debt consolidation, in which all your bills are paid by one lender, who then becomes the only creditor you owe money to.

Chapter 15

Your Emotions and Credit

It is a subject that few people discuss, but more and more therapists are talking about it - the key link between our emotions and our money. We may think that money is all about our rational selves, but in fact, our emotions are often very much invested in our pocket books.

If we want to repair our credit, we have to deal with the emotional as well as the numerical side of money. There are a few tips that financial experts now believe can help you harness your emotions in a way that can help you improve your credit score:

Give Yourself a Break

There is no point in beating yourself up over your credit score - whatever it is. Instead, promise yourself that you will do better in the future and then work to repair your credit rather than working on berating yourself. Taking action to improve your credit rating will improve your outlook as well as your credit.

Don't Make Excuses

If you have been the object of identity theft or have genuinely been mistreated by a company, then include an explanatory note in your credit report. However, most lenders do not want to hear a lot of excuses. Whatever your problems have been in the past, you will seem like a much more reliable lender if you focus on what you are doing to get out of problems.

You will feel better and get better responses from lenders if your focus on current action rather than past mistakes. Instead of wallowing in pity and explaining in great detail the personal and financial problems that led to a bad credit rating, give yourself and lenders the condensed version and then move on to a detailed review of what you are doing to repair your credit.

Give Yourself a Treat - Without Affecting Your Credit Rating

Reestablishing good credit is hard work and daunting as well. Occasionally, as you reach a milestone, you need to reward yourself. You should do this through some means that do not involve debt or money. If you repay your credit card bill, there is no sense in running up that bill again on a shopping trip.

Instead, you should list some inexpensive and fun treats you could give yourself. Keep this list wherever you keep your financial file. As you reach a big milestone, take out your list and immediately reward yourself with one of the items on the list. This will not only keep you motivated, but it will inexpensively keep you from feeling too deprived while you work on your credit score.

Work on Your Emotional Response To Debt And Money

Most of us carry a lot of emotional baggage with us when it comes to money. We see money as a marker of success, or we see money as a way of making ourselves feel better, and these attitudes lead us to much of our financial and credit problems. If we rely on money to make us feel successful, then we are apt to overspend. If we fear money - or the lack of it - we are unlikely to save it or make investments with it.

We need to be aware of the ways we respond to money and the ways that those responses shape the ways we deal with money. Some financial experts recommend that clients keep money journals, in which they record their money hopes, their money fears, and their responses to spending and money. A money journal can help you by showing you how to feel about spending and about money. If you can isolate the emotions that influence how you spend money and how you make your money decisions, you will be well on your way towards fixing your financial problems.

Don't Mix Debt with Emotion And Stay Aware Of Your Emotions

It pays to separate your feelings of worth and your

emotions from your finances, especially when you are trying to repair your credit. Feeling self-pity, shame, fear, or sadness as you try to repair your credit score won't help you. Staying calm and professional as you deal with credit bureaus and financial professionals will help you. If you need to, keep telling yourself that your credit score is just an important number. Keep it separate from yourself and your emotional state as far as possible.

Bad credit can be emotionally trying, and boosting your credit can be daunting and difficult as well. It is important that you keep track of your emotions during the process. If you find yourself dwelling on your credit too much or if you find yourself severely depressed, seek help at once. A credit problem is a fixable solution - do not let it become an emotional disaster for you.

Get Help If You Need It

Do not be afraid to ask for help - financial or emotional - if you need it. There are a number of wonderful organizations that can help you if a problem is causing your credit problems. If you have credit problems due to compulsive overspending, for example, Over Spenders Anonymous (OSA) can be a great help.

If you suffer from a gambling problem, there are many charitable organizations that can help you overcome the addiction. If you have accumulated debt because of these sorts of specific problems, you will not really be able to fix your credit rating unless you deal with the problems behind the bad credit. Many good groups and therapists out there can help you.

Find a recommendation for a good one from your family doctor or a trusted friend or family member. You will be glad that you did.

Chapter 16

Credit Tips

Before you head off to enjoy your new and improved credit score or to work on boosting your credit score, consider two more tips that may well come in handy as you try to repair your credit score:

Learn to Deal with Collection Agencies

If you have bad credit, you will have to deal with collection agencies sooner or later, and these companies often present the most persistent and unpleasant problem for those with bad credit. Collection agencies are basically companies that work on behalf of companies to try to recoup money that is owed.

If you owe your credit card company a payment that has not been made in some time, your credit card company will eventually ask a collection agency to speak with you. In many cases, collection agencies try to get money for their clients through phone calls. Some collection agencies are quite reasonable and will try to work with you. However, some will use threatening or harassing techniques - including verbal threats and daily phone calls - to try to get you to pay. To prevent the stress that collection agencies can cause, learn to deal with collection agencies.

You should always get the full name of whomever you speak with at a collection agency. You should try to be honest about your ability to repay and try to work out a payment schedule or payment options. If at any point you feel threatened or harassed, say so. Hang up the phone if the collection agent persists and contact the company who is trying to recoup money from you directly.

Note that the collection agency the company uses has been using abusive or upsetting language and ask to resolve the issue with someone at the company directly. Get the name of the collection agency and report them - and the agent you spoke with - to the Better Business Bureau. Refuse further calls from the collection agency and continue your communication with the creditor directly, noting each time the collection company contacts you with harassing or abusive calls.

Unfortunately, some collection agencies feel that intimidation yields the best results and since most collection agencies work through telephoning, they feel that they can say whatever they like (including making personal and false accusations) in order to try to recoup money for their clients. There is no paper trail and few people harassed by the agencies take these companies to court.

Some debtors feel so ashamed of their bad credit rating that they almost feel that they deserve the abuse. Both views are completely wrong. A bad credit rating does not make you deserving of abuse. Report collection agencies that offer harassment as a technique and make it clear to lenders that you will not work with a company that uses abuse as a technique of recouping money.

Some collection agencies will try to use your credit score against you, telling you that they can ruin your credit score at a glance or file a claim on your credit score. Don't fall for this. Your credit score is instantly affected when you fail to make a payment or are reported to a collection agency, but there is nothing that the collection agency employee can do to make your credit score worse beyond those two things.

You will still be eligible for credit in many cases. Do not let false claims about your credit score intimidate you into accepting the abuse of a collection agency.

Keep at It

Credit repair is not something that you simply do once in a while when your credit rating slips below 620. Credit repair and credit check-ups need to be part of your overall long-term financial plan. You need to follow a regular maintenance schedule of checking your credit reports regularly (you can get one free credit report from each of the major credit bureaus every four months, which lets you check your credit for free three times a year).

Regular check-ups will ensure that you have not been the victim of identity theft and will help you make sure that your credit has not begun to slip. Catching errors and problems early can be an excellent long-term way to ensure that you never need intensive credit repair again.

Your credit should be part of your financial goals because your credit can help you meet your goals. Good credit can help make loans affordable, and so can help make education, homes, and cars possible.

Your credit score will not stay steady - it may drop due to oversight or if you suddenly open some new loan accounts. However, overall you should continue to follow the strategies in this book in order to develop good habits that will keep your financial life stable and will help keep your credit score overall in good repair.

Conclusion

If you follow all - or even some - of these tips, you will notice an improvement in your credit rating with time. The main thing is to keep showing lenders that you are a good credit risk and keeping your credit report safe from identity thieves and hackers. If you already suffer from bad credit, developing your own method of credit repair using the tips in this book can help you reestablish the credit risk rating that can get you the best interest rates possible.

In general, you will want to follow at least four steps to better credit scores:

1) Check your credit report and credit scores. Assess your current situation and make sure to correct any errors on your report by writing to the credit bureaus and the creditors involved. Immediately report any charges you don't recognize - these may indicate an error, but they might also indicate that you have been the victim of fraud or identity theft.

2) Pay down your debts and pay your bills on time. Close the shorter-term loans if you need to.

3) Do all you can to make good financial habits automatic to keep your credit rating good.

4) Address issues - such as too much debt or a student lifestyle - that you think may be contributing to your low credit rating.

Developing your own plan for credit repair is the most cost-effective and often the most efficient way of dealing with bad credit. It also gives you the tools, knowledge, and self-confidence to take control of your finances and ensure that you get the best credit score you can.

By being persistent and following the tips in this book, you can turn your credit situation around. With your new, good credit score, you can become qualified for that great new job, that apartment, or the fabulous interest rate on that loan you need. With a great credit rating, your financial life will be much easier.

You have all the tools and resources in this book to start repairing your credit right now. You can use the tools presented here to follow your financial dreams and achieve the success you deserve. So, start reestablishing your credit so that you can live the life you want right now!

www.ingramcontent.com/pod-product-compliance
Lightning Source LLC
Chambersburg PA
CBHW021950170526
45157CB00003B/929